MEET THE DINOSAURS!: WHEN REPTILES RULED

MEET THE SMALL DINOSAURS

by Rebecca Donnelly
illustrated by Alan Brown

GRASSHOPPER

Tools for Parents & Teachers

Grasshopper Books enhance imagination and introduce the earliest readers to fiction with fun storylines and illustrations. The easy-to-read text supports early reading experiences with repetitive sentence patterns and sight words.

Before Reading

- Discuss the cover illustration. What do they see?
- Look at the glossary together. Discuss the words.

Read the Book

- Read the book to the child, or have him or her read independently.
- "Walk" through the book and look at the illustrations. What is happening in the story?

After Reading

- Prompt the child to think more. Ask: The size and shape of a dinosaur's teeth can tell you what it eats. What do the teeth of the small dinosaurs in this book look like? Can you tell what they ate by looking at their teeth?

Grasshopper Books are published by Jump!
5357 Penn Avenue South
Minneapolis, MN 55419
www.jumplibrary.com

Library of Congress Cataloging-in-Publication Data

Names: Donnelly, Rebecca, author.
Brown, Alan, illustrator.
Title: Meet the small dinosaurs / Rebecca Donnelly;
illustrated by Alan Brown.
Description: Minneapolis, MN: Jump!, Inc., [2022]
Series: Meet the dinosaurs!: when reptiles ruled
Includes index.
Audience: Ages 7-10
Identifiers: LCCN 2021038053 (print)
LCCN 2021038054 (ebook)
ISBN 9781636906171 (hardcover)
ISBN 9781636906188 (paperback)
ISBN 9781636906195 (ebook)
Subjects: LCSH: Dinosaurs–Size–Juvenile literature.
Classification: LCC QE861.5 .D6847 2022 (print)
LCC QE861.5 (ebook)
DDC 567.9–dc23
LC record available at https://lccn.loc.gov/2021038053
LC ebook record available at https://lccn.loc.gov/2021038054

Editor: Eliza Leahy
Direction and Layout: Anna Peterson
Illustrator: Alan Brown

Printed in the United States of America at
Corporate Graphics in North Mankato, Minnesota.

Table of Contents

Small but Mighty

Hi, I'm Dan the Dilong! I'm the meanest, scariest dinosaur you'll ever meet—if you're a small lizard! So what if I'm less than 5 feet (1.5 meters) long?

My teeth are made for tearing meat, and my legs are made for running. Little dinosaurs like me might not look as impressive as the big guys, but we're just as good at hunting. Speaking of hunting, gotta go!

I'm Polly the Procompsognathus. I'm just 3.5 feet (1.1 m) long. You might think that's too small to be a mighty carnivore. But my prey is tiny, too. This cockroach is tasty!

Luke the Lesothosaurus is my name! I'm about the same size as Polly, but I'm an herbivore. My small teeth grind plant leaves and stems.

I don't chase my food, but I still have to be fast to escape predators!

Hi, I'm Betsy. I'm a Bambiraptor. I'm only 3 feet (0.9 m) long. I weigh less than 5 pounds (2.3 kilograms). But that doesn't stop me from catching food! I wound my prey with my sharp claw.

claw

I'm Mei the Microraptor. I only weigh 2.5 pounds (1.1 kg), but I'm a great hunter. I can do something a lot of other dinosaurs can't. I can hunt from the air!

My wings and feathers help me glide.
That mammal looks tasty. *Swoosh!*

I’m Joe the Juravenator.
I’m just 2.5 feet (0.8 m) long.
I’m a fast runner.

I have another hunting trick, too. Fish are one of my favorite meals. I have special scales on my tail that help me find them underwater. I use my tail to sense their movement.

Gotcha!

I’m Winnie the Wannanosaurus.
I’m the size of a small dog.

I’m the smallest Pachycephalosaurus. We all have hard heads! My skull is super thick, but I don’t use it as a weapon. It’s just a cool way to show off how unique I am. I eat plants like these ferns. Yum!

My name is Avery the Aquilops. I weigh just 4 pounds (1.8 kg). That's about the size of a rabbit. But I'm not cuddly.

My beak is sharp. It helps me eat tough plants. I have to be careful around dinosaurs and mammals that eat little critters like me!

beak

Psst, down here! It's me, the smallest dinosaur of all, Payton the Parvicursor. I'm just 12 inches (30 centimeters) long.

I'm a carnivore. I like to eat termites. Delicious! Who needs to be big? My small friends and I may be extinct now, but we had a lot going for us!

Timeline

Dinosaurs lived millions of years ago. Take a look at when the dinosaurs in this book lived!

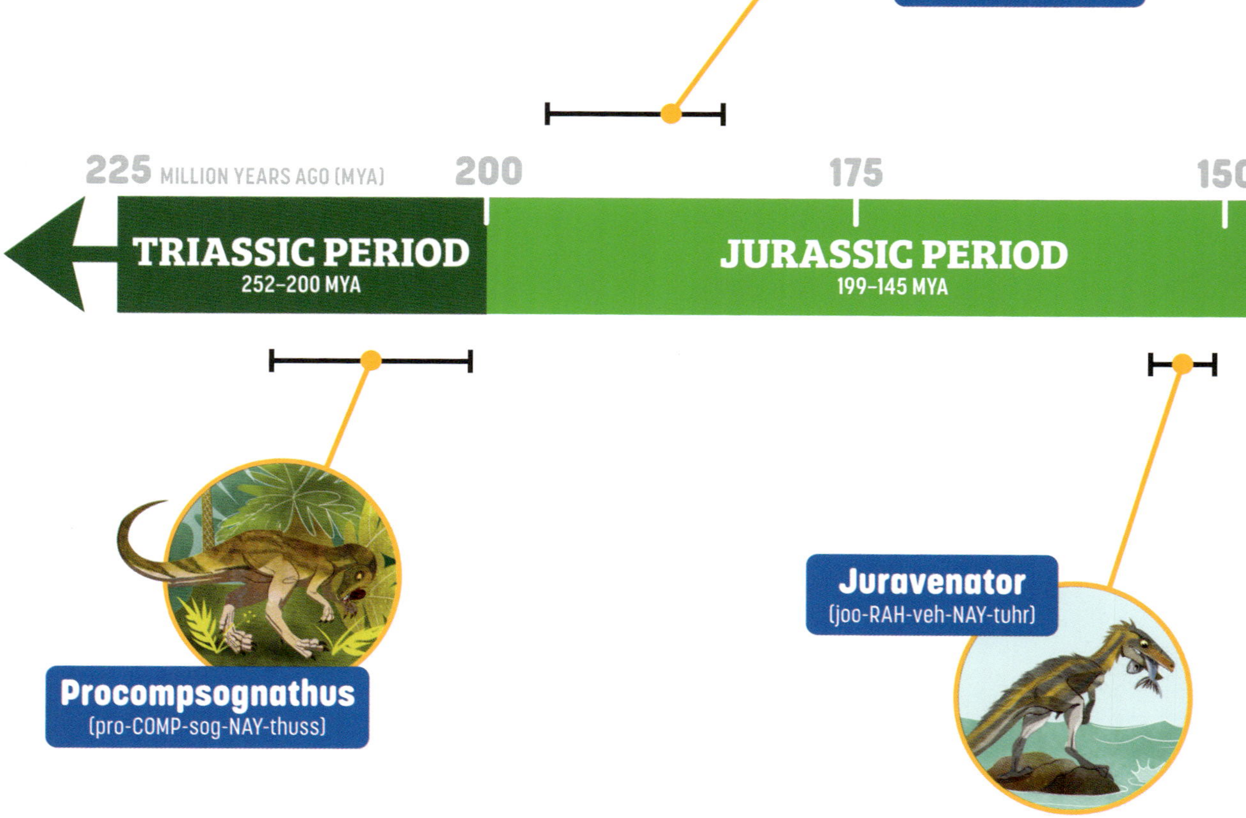

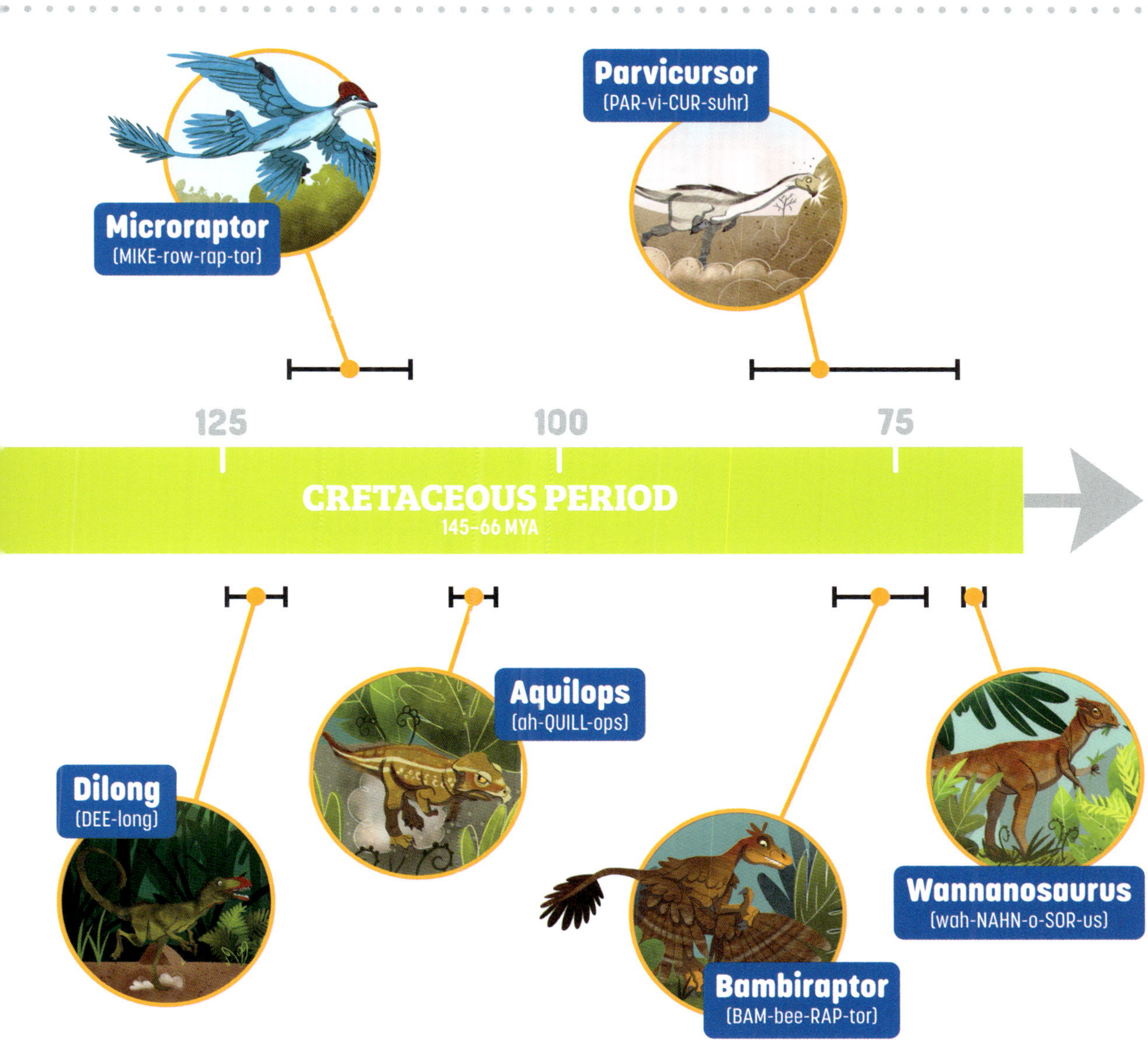
Microraptor
(MIKE-row-rap-tor)
Parvicursor
(PAR-vi-CUR-suhr)
125
100
75
CRETACEOUS PERIOD
145–66 MYA
Dilong
(DEE-long)
Aquilops
(ah-QUILL-ops)
Bambiraptor
(BAM-bee-RAP-tor)
Wannanosaurus
(wah-NAHN-o-SOR-us)

Glossary

carnivore: An animal that eats meat.

extinct: No longer found alive and known about only through fossils or history.

herbivore: An animal that eats plants.

mammal: A warm-blooded animal that gives birth to live young.

Pachycephalosaurus: A type of dinosaur with thick skull bones.

predators: Animals that hunt other animals for food.

prey: Animals that are hunted by other animals for food.

scales: Thin, flat, overlapping pieces of hard skin that cover the bodies of reptiles.

wound: To cause injury.

Index

To Learn More

Finding more information is as easy as 1, 2, 3.

1. Go to www.factsurfer.com
2. Enter "**meetthesmalldinosaurs**" into the search box.
3. Choose your book to see a list of websites.

FACT SURFER